BUCKET LIST
JOURNAL

Create a Lifetime of
Inspiration and
Purpose

To my sister Kate,
whom I hope lives a very rich and full life.

BUCKET LIST JOURNAL

Create a Lifetime of
Inspiration and
Purpose

Alex Wagman

ROCK
POINT

Quarto is the authority on a wide range of topics.

Quarto educates, entertains and enriches the lives of
our readers—enthusiasts and lovers of hands-on living.

www.quartoknows.com

A division of Quarto Publishing Group USA Inc.

142 West 36th Street, 4th Floor

New York, New York 10018

quartoknows.com

ROCK POINT and the distinctive Rock Point logo are trademarks of
Quarto Publishing Group USA Inc.

© 2015 Rock Point

Interior design & Illustration by Monica Gurevich

ISBN-13: 978-1-63106-057-1

Printed in China

2 4 6 8 10 9 7 5 3

Table of Contents

INTRODUCTION

"Those who dream by night in the dusty recesses of their minds
wake in the day to find that all was vanity: but the dreamers of
the day are dangerous men, for they may act their
dream with open eyes, and make it possible."
—T.E. LAWRENCE

Imagine this: Every morning upon waking up, a generous donor credits your bank account with $86,400. You are allowed to spend the cash however you like, but none of it carries over from one day to the next, and you're not allowed to save anything that wasn't spent. How much would you withdraw and spend each day? Every cent, of course. Well, what if I told you that you have such a benefactor and bank account, but its name is "life" and the currency is "time." Every morning it credits you with 86,400 seconds, and every night it writes off whatever amount you failed to invest to good purpose—no overdrafts and no extensions of credit. Whatever you choose to do today is exceedingly important because you are exchanging 86,400 seconds of your life for it. If you fail to use today's deposit, the loss is yours. So how much does your "bank statement" say that you have withdrawn this week? Are you investing every penny that you are given, and are you spending it so as to get the highest return-on-investment in health, happiness, and meaning? Your life is a gift, so make sure that you treasure it and give it back with plenty of interest. The clock is running.

Five Great Reasons to Start a Bucket List

1 A bucket list will **help you repossess your enthusiasm for life.** Getting started on any project or goal requires finding a way to overcome inertia with motivation. Drawing up your own personal bucket list can serve as an excellent catalyst for kick-starting these goals, as it provides you with a new sense of meaning and purpose.

2 A bucket list will **make your goals more manageable.** The human mind operates more efficiently when it has a list of specific goals to work toward, and writing down your goals will help you focus more on the tasks at hand. Doesn't it make sense that life will seem more manageable when thought of as a scavenger hunt as opposed to a surprise party?

3 A bucket list will **keep you accountable for and mindful of what you want out of life.** Keeping a journal where the goals are readily visible is the first step toward turning them into a reality. Do you ever make a to-do list? Isn't it true that the more you look at the list, the quicker those things get done? Well, it works the same way with goals. Compiling your list will prevent further procrastination and keep you responsible for actualizing your dreams.

4 A bucket list will **prompt you to discover your true potential.** As you document your victories and your progress, you will find yourself reaching further than you normally would. You will never know your full potential until you push yourself to find it, and it is this self-discovery that will inevitably take you to the wildest places on earth.

5 Fulfillment of a bucket list will **ultimately bring you more happiness!** The key to a happier life is contained in the dreams that you already have, and when these dreams turn into realities, the immediate emotion that results is happiness. Achieving your goals can create motivation, independence, and meaning; it can also strengthen relationships, assure self-improvement, and bring joy.

How to Approach This Journal

MOST BOOKS ARE WRITTEN TO ENTERTAIN OR TO INFORM; THIS BOOK IS WRITTEN TO INSPIRE. Too often, bucket lists are pre-packaged and handed down as "one size fits all," but this journal has been created so that you can dream up destinations, record your wildest passions, and check off all of your adventures—all on your own terms. Use this journal to find the joy in your life and write down any thoughts, comments, or cherished quotes that come to mind in the blank space provided. Think of the blank space in each section as a blueprint for your own "life list," and think of the text as additional inspiration to point you in the right direction with examples to help get you started.

Remember, no two bucket lists are alike, but each list has the same end goal: to remind you that time is precious, and whatever you decide to do with your time should be thought out very carefully. Try to maintain the mindset that crossing everything off of your list may be impossible, but have the courage to uphold "complete accomplishment" as the model.

This *Bucket List Journal* is much more than a standard checklist. In fact, the completion of this journal will result in several different works; it will stand as a memoir, an epic poem, and an unfinished adventure novel, all rolled into one.

Start off strong and remember that "well begun is half done."
Be steadfast in your journey, be bold in your pursuit, and with everything you do, remember to live out your dreams so that they are more than just a bucket list.

COMPASSION
BUCKET LIST

CHAPTER 1

Many bucket listers who are searching for greatness tend to choose something like skydiving or paragliding as their first course of action, but I prefer a different approach. If you want to achieve true greatness through your bucket list, I recommend that you first begin with goodness. That's where the Compassion Bucket List comes in. This list is based on the idea that wherever there is a human being, there will also be an opportunity to serve someone with kindness. This list is not designed to force yourself into sainthood but to stretch what you think you are capable of in terms of compassion and loving kindness.

One of my favorite features of this list is that you don't have to wait for just the right moment in your life to achieve these goals. Living with kindness and compassion can begin right now. We all have two of the most valuable things that can be offered in compassion: time and attention. If you have an irrepressible desire to live until you can be assured that the world is a little better for your having lived in it, then this bucket list is especially for you. Regardless of whether you attempt to perform an act of kindness every day or not, my hope is that you will join in the pursuit of good deeds, acts of generosity, works of kindness, and ways to love, not just in your day-to-day motions but through your overall attitude and motivations as well. The power of kindness is immense. Really, it is nothing less than the power to change the world.

NOW IT'S YOUR TURN. HOW CAN YOU HELP OTHERS?

Here are some examples to help get you started:

* Pay for someone else's meal

* Send a letter to a teacher or professor you once had and let him or her know about the difference he or she has made in your life

* Pick up the next piece of litter you see on the sidewalk

* Volunteer at a soup kitchen

* Donate blood

* Surprise someone with coffee and a pastry

* Get in touch with an old friend

* Send a care package to a soldier

* Try to make somebody laugh

* Offer up a compliment to a stranger

* Leave a very generous tip

* Help someone in distress

* Visit a neighbor with a bouquet of flowers for no reason at all

* Offer to do the grocery shopping for a disabled or elderly neighbor

* If you are the boss, bring your assistant a cup of coffee in the morning

* Recognize and praise the work or attitude of a person you work with

* Bake a delicious pie for a close friend and leave it on his or her doorstep with a note

Compassion Bucket List

Who Can I Help _____

How Can I Help _____

_____

The World Is Now a Happier Place ⭕

· · · · · · · · · · · · · · · · · · ·

Who Can I Help _____

How Can I Help _____

_____

The World Is Now a Happier Place ⭕

· · · · · · · · · · · · · · · · · · ·

Who Can I Help _____

How Can I Help _____

_____

The World Is Now a Happier Place ⭕

Compassion Bucket List

Who Can I Help _____

How Can I Help _____

_____

The World Is Now a Happier Place ◯

· · · · · · · · · · · · · · · · · ·

Who Can I Help _____

How Can I Help _____

_____

The World Is Now a Happier Place ◯

· · · · · · · · · · · · · · · · · ·

Who Can I Help _____

How Can I Help _____

_____

The World Is Now a Happier Place ◯

Compassion Bucket List

Who Can I Help _____

How Can I Help _____

_____

The World Is Now a Happier Place ◯

· · · · · · · · · · · · · · · · · · ·

Who Can I Help _____

How Can I Help _____

_____

The World Is Now a Happier Place ◯

· · · · · · · · · · · · · · · · · · ·

Who Can I Help _____

How Can I Help _____

_____

The World Is Now a Happier Place ◯

Compassion Bucket List

Who Can I Help _____

How Can I Help _____

_____

The World Is Now a Happier Place ◯

• • • • • • • • • • • • • • • • • •

Who Can I Help _____

How Can I Help _____

_____

The World Is Now a Happier Place ◯

• • • • • • • • • • • • • • • • •

Who Can I Help _____

How Can I Help _____

_____

The World Is Now a Happier Place ◯

Compassion Bucket List

Who Can I Help _____

How Can I Help _____

_____

The World Is Now a Happier Place ◯

· · · · · · · · · · · · · · · · · · · ·

Who Can I Help _____

How Can I Help _____

_____

The World Is Now a Happier Place ◯

· · · · · · · · · · · · · · · · · · · ·

Who Can I Help _____

How Can I Help _____

_____

The World Is Now a Happier Place ◯

Compassion Bucket List

Who Can I Help _____

How Can I Help _____

_____

The World Is Now a Happier Place ◯

· · · · · · · · · · · · · · · · · ·

Who Can I Help _____

How Can I Help _____

_____

The World Is Now a Happier Place ◯

· · · · · · · · · · · · · · · · · ·

Who Can I Help _____

How Can I Help _____

_____

The World Is Now a Happier Place ◯

Compassion Bucket List

Who Can I Help _____

How Can I Help _____

_____

The World Is Now a Happier Place ◯

· ·

Who Can I Help _____

How Can I Help _____

_____

The World Is Now a Happier Place ◯

· ·

Who Can I Help _____

How Can I Help _____

_____

The World Is Now a Happier Place ◯

LEARNING BUCKET LIST

CHAPTER 2

Take a minute and think about what you have learned today. What information have you absorbed, what lessons have you encountered, and what skills have you picked up? No matter your age, there's always something new to learn, and there's always room for you to expand your life and your mind with new knowledge and experiences. One of the main reasons that I encourage a Learning Bucket List is because it always keeps bucket listers moving forward and often serves as a spark plug for acquiring knowledge. Regardless of whether or not you know how to complete something on your list, the motivation of crossing everything off will drive you to teach yourself; plus, hands-on experience and self-driven adventure can often be the best way to learn something new.

When drawing up your own Learning Bucket List, it is important to maintain a passionate curiosity and an insatiable appetite for whatever it is that you seek to learn. If you have a question, don't wait for someone to explain the answer to you; go out and capture the information on your own. So what is it that you would like to learn today, and what's holding you back from getting started? There are so many different ways to educate oneself, so don't limit yourself to just one. Whether you travel somewhere new, read a chapter of a book, or just kick back and watch a new documentary, you can be assured that you will know more about the world today than you knew yesterday. Learning something new can be both a timeless pleasure and an invaluable treasure, so make sure that you never exhaust your propensity to learn and always desire more knowledge than you can take in.

Here are some great ways to kick-start your life of learning:

* ✳ Sign up for a dance class

* ✳ Attend a basic self-defense class

* ✳ Become familiar with the compositions of Bach, Beethoven, and Debussy

* ✳ Learn to play the piano by ear

* ✳ Read something by Shakespeare, Twain, Hemingway, Dickens, and Poe

* ✳ Learn glassblowing

* ✳ Read a book about a time in history that you know very little about

I WANT TO LEARN _more about WWII_

WHY _to build my repetoire of knowledge_

WHEN _By summer 2017_ ☺

HOW _Lots of research and library trips!_

I TRULY AM SMARTER AND WISER TODAY THAN I WAS YESTERDAY ◯

• • • • • • • • • • • • • •

I WANT TO LEARN

WHY

WHEN

HOW

I TRULY AM SMARTER AND WISER TODAY THAN I WAS YESTERDAY ◯

Learning Bucket List

I want to learn _____

Why _____

When _____

How _____

I truly am smarter and wiser today than I was yesterday ⭕

· · · · · · · · · · · · ·

I want to learn _____

Why _____

When _____

How _____

I truly am smarter and wiser today than I was yesterday ⭕

Learning Bucket List

I WANT TO LEARN _____

WHY _____

WHEN _____

HOW _____

I TRULY AM SMARTER AND WISER TODAY THAN I WAS YESTERDAY ◯

• • • • • • • • • • • • • • • •

I WANT TO LEARN _____

WHY _____

WHEN _____

HOW _____

I TRULY AM SMARTER AND WISER TODAY THAN I WAS YESTERDAY ◯

Learning Bucket List

I want to learn _____

WHY _____

WHEN _____

HOW _____

I truly am smarter and wiser today than I was yesterday ○

· · · · · · · · · · · · · · ·

I want to learn _____

WHY _____

WHEN _____

HOW _____

I truly am smarter and wiser today than I was yesterday ○

Learning Bucket List

I want to learn _____

WHY _____

WHEN _____

HOW _____

I truly am smarter and wiser today than I was yesterday ◯

• • • • • • • • • • • • • • • •

I want to learn _____

WHY _____

WHEN _____

HOW _____

I truly am smarter and wiser today than I was yesterday ◯

Learning Bucket List

I WANT TO LEARN _____

WHY _____

WHEN _____

HOW _____

I TRULY AM SMARTER AND WISER TODAY THAN I WAS YESTERDAY ○

. . . .

I WANT TO LEARN _____

WHY _____

WHEN _____

HOW _____

I TRULY AM SMARTER AND WISER TODAY THAN I WAS YESTERDAY ○

Learning Bucket List

I WANT TO LEARN _____

WHY _____

WHEN _____

HOW _____

I TRULY AM SMARTER AND WISER TODAY THAN I WAS YESTERDAY ◯

· · · · · · · · · · · · · · · ·

I WANT TO LEARN _____

WHY _____

WHEN _____

HOW _____

I TRULY AM SMARTER AND WISER TODAY THAN I WAS YESTERDAY ◯

OBSESSION BUCKET LIST

CHAPTER 3

Contrary to what you might believe, you have a "calling." In fact, all of us have in our hearts an image of the person we can be and the life we can live. We all have natural talents and aspirations to capitalize on, and we all have a project or interest that we feel intrinsically rewarded by. Although I believe it is important to lead a dynamic life with a slew of interests and hobbies, I also believe that it is important to find one that you want to excel at. Mastery is a form of power and intelligence that represents the highest form of human potential. It is the source of the greatest achievements and discoveries in history, and it requires an intellect and bullheadedness that is not taught in schools nor analyzed by professors.

To become an expert of your obsession, you must devote plenty of attention and tenacity to whatever that one obsession is, and make pleasure a by-product rather than the end goal as you work. Ask yourself what makes you come alive and go do that, because what the world needs is not more salary-seeking professionals, but more people who are doing what they love. Since willingness to practice is the most important element in developing an area of expertise, you should prize your enthusiasm even more than your innate ability. Your obsession should be the kind of work that makes you lose track of time and gives you so much gratification that you would choose to do that work even if you won the lottery tomorrow. So follow your bliss and get obsessed. Become a proficient, innovative, forward-looking fanatic, and build something in your area of interest that will outlast you.

Here are some helpful tips to get you started:

* Put a deadline on your next step to challenge and motivate yourself

* Include a list of obstacles that you may have to overcome

* Find a famous quote that will inspire you to overcome these obstacles

* Find a mentor in your field of interest and draw from his or her well of experience

Obsession Bucket List

WHAT DO YOU PLAN TO DO WITH YOUR ONE WILD AND
PRECIOUS LIFE?

Obsession Bucket List

WHAT MAKES YOU COME ALIVE? WHY?

Obsession Bucket List

WHAT MAKES YOU COME ALIVE? WHY?

Obsession Bucket List

WHAT IS YOUR ULTIMATE GOAL IN THIS PURSUIT?

Obsession Bucket List

WHAT DO YOU NEED TO DO TO ACCOMPLISH YOUR ULTIMATE GOAL?

Obsession Bucket List

LIST OF NEXT STEPS: · DEADLINE:

NOTES:

Gratitude Bucket List

CHAPTER 4

If you haven't already noticed, life can get away from us even while we are still living it. Sometimes we focus on the milestones too much, and as a result, we forget to appreciate all of the precious little moments. Life isn't just about the professional achievements, the graduations, and the passing of age; it's also about the lazy Sunday afternoons, the bowls of cereal eaten together, and hot cups of tea on a cold day. These are the things that help keep our lives balanced and prevent us from being crushed under the weight of seriousness. Sure, there is always work to be done around the house or in the office, but finding enjoyment in life is so much more important, healthy—and fun. I will always encourage setting new goals and searching for the next bucket list adventure, but in between the goals is a thing called life, and it must be appreciated and admired with all of its simple amusements.

I have compiled a list of some simple amusements that I am grateful for, and I encourage you to do the same. This new approach is about focusing on the things that already bring you happiness. It's about living with such respect and reverence for life that you approach each day with a sincere "thank you" poised on your lips. I often flip through my own Gratitude Bucket List as a reminder to be more thankful, or in order to give myself a reason to cheer up. It doesn't matter whether it rains or shines, if you are experiencing intense hardship, or you just need a pick-me-up, because these small blessings are already yours—they are only awaiting your recognition. I'm giving you the beginning of my list in the hope that you will find, as I did, that happiness comes from noticing and enjoying the little things in life. Such soul food has been at our fingertips all along. Now it's up to you to slow down, kickback, and enjoy!

Here are 20 things to be grateful for:

* Holding hands in the car

* Viewing a sky full of stars with your back on the ground

* Watching home videos with family and friends

* Getting things done way before the deadline

* The smell of puppy breath

* The feeling of release after a highly anticipated sneeze

* Singing along to a throwback song in the car

* Having a dog that always greets you at the door

* A gentle kiss on the back of your neck

* An unexpected "yes"

* Finally remembering that one thing on the tip of your tongue

* Having the family together after being apart for a long time

* The first scoop out of a jar of peanut butter

* The moment on vacation when you forget what day of the week it is

* People-watching from a park bench

* Sleeping in new bed sheets

* Sunday naps

* Arriving at your destination just as a great song ends

* The imagination of a three-year-old child

* The first fog of winter and the first flower of spring

Gratitude Bucket List

CREATE A LIST OF 100 THINGS TO BE GRATEFUL FOR:

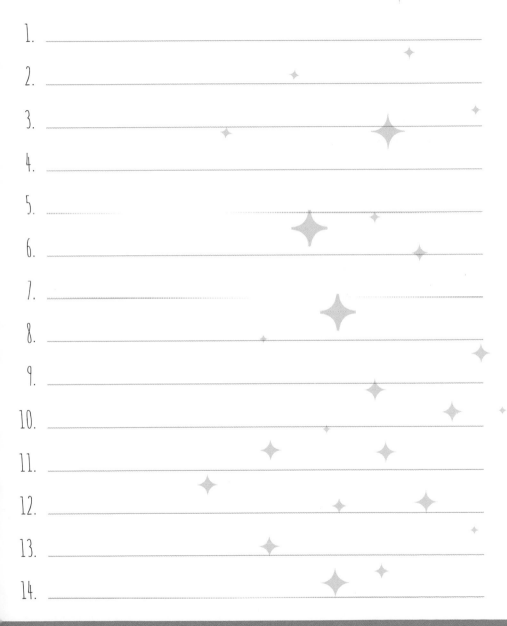

1.
2.
3.
4.
5.
6.
7.
8.
9.
10.
11.
12.
13.
14.

Gratitude Bucket List

15. _____

16. _____

17. _____

18. _____

19. _____

20. _____

21. _____

22. _____

23. _____

24. _____

25. _____

26. _____

27. _____

28. _____

Gratitude Bucket List

29. _____

30. _____

31. _____

32. _____

33. _____

34. _____

35. _____

35. _____

36. _____

37. _____

38. _____

39. _____

40. _____

41. _____

Gratitude Bucket List

43. _____

44. _____

45. _____

46. _____

47. _____

48. _____

49. _____

50. _____

51. _____

52. _____

53. _____

54. _____

55. _____

56. _____

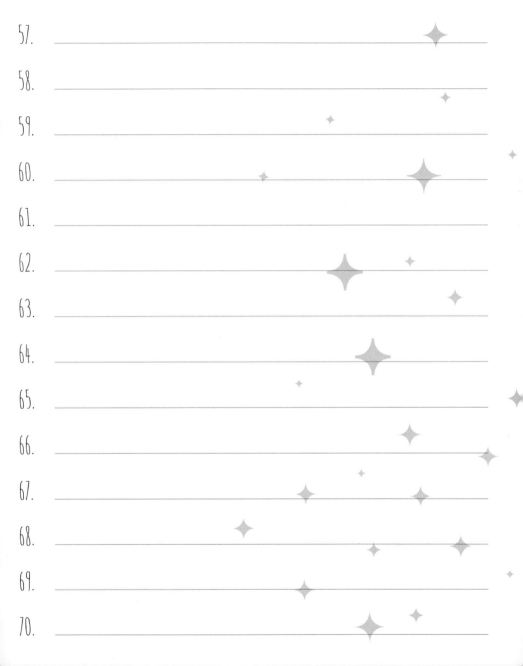

Gratitude Bucket List

57. _____

58. _____

59. _____

60. _____

61. _____

62. _____

63. _____

64. _____

65. _____

66. _____

67. _____

68. _____

69. _____

70. _____

Gratitude Bucket List

71. _____

72. _____

73. _____

74. _____

75. _____

76. _____

77. _____

78. _____

79. _____

80. _____

81. _____

82. _____

83. _____

84. _____

85. _____

Gratitude Bucket List

86. _____

87. _____

88. _____

89. _____

90. _____

91. _____

92. _____

93. _____

94. _____

95. _____

96. _____

97. _____

98. _____

99. _____

100. _____

Spiritual Bucket List

CHAPTER 5

What if there was an actual bucket list that was designed specifically for you since the beginning of time? An agenda of adventures that you were made to experience and a lifestyle that you were meant to live before you kicked the proverbial bucket? Well, the basic idea behind keeping a bucket list in the first place is for our souls to desire something greater. I believe that we are meant to desire something greater simply because we are meant to be satisfied by something greater—something beyond the physical, something that is spiritual.

You may imagine that seeking and submitting to a life of spirituality might be limiting, unappealing, and could translate into becoming a sequestered nun, a missionary in Ethiopia, or something else contrary to the dreams you have already written down up to this point. As members of the human race, we have been given an incredible mission here on earth: to charter and explore, build, conquer, and individually care for different things in all of creation. Whether you build a boat and sail it, write a symphony and play it, or plant a field and care for it, any desire will ultimately put you more in touch with your soul and spiritual life.

So don't suppress any of these desires that you may have, but embrace them. The key to this grand way of living life is to submit to something greater than yourself while listening to the desires of your heart at the same time. Throughout this book, I want to urge you to develop yourself to the fullest, and I don't think that this can happen when the spiritual part of life is ignored. This list will help you pursue life with intention and purpose rather than by chance and coincidence. So let your desires endure, let your passions persist, and make sure to live a life that is ultimately driven by eternity.

Here are some helpful ideas to get you started :

* Meditate for the next five days and see how it affects the rest of your week

* Think of your toughest spiritual conflict and then research and resolve it

* Attend a religious ceremony or service for at least three different religions in order to challenge yourself spiritually

* Finish reading a holy book from cover to cover

* Strike up a spiritual conversation with someone you know

* Spend a weekend with monks in a monastery

* Serve as an elder or leader in a holy service

* Visit the Vatican

* Learn to pray

* Devote at least an hour of your week toward a spiritual devotional group

* Fast for a day

Spiritual Bucket List

TIP:

Be able to answer spiritual questions such as the following:

Why is there suffering in the world?

Is there life after death?

What is the meaning of life?

Which experiences do you want to define your spiritual journey?

Spiritual Goals

Spiritual Bucket List

Spiritual Goals _____

_____

_____

_____

_____

_____

_____

_____

_____

_____

_____

_____

_____

Spiritual Bucket List

Spiritual Goals _____

_____

_____

_____

_____

_____

_____

_____

_____

_____

_____

_____

_____

_____

_____

_____

_____

Spiritual Bucket List

Spiritual Goals

Spiritual Bucket List

Spiritual Goals _____

_____

_____

_____

_____

_____

_____

_____

_____

_____

_____

_____

_____

_____

_____

_____

_____

Spiritual Bucket List

Spiritual Goals _____

_____

_____

_____

_____

_____

_____

_____

_____

_____

_____

_____

_____

Spiritual Bucket List

Spiritual Goals _____

_____

_____

_____

_____

_____

_____

_____

_____

_____

_____

_____

_____

_____

_____

Everyday Adventure Bucket List

CHAPTER 6

Want to get the most out of your life? Then look at it as an adventure. If you embrace adventure in your social, educational, spiritual, professional, and recreational lives, you will never say the words "I'm bored" again. The kind of adventure that I'm referring to in this instance is not the type that has you cliff-top camping in the Alps or stranded in the middle of the jungle. No, the kind of adventure that will help you get the most out of life is the adventure that will force you to step out of your routine and encourage you to find simple ways to live uniquely.

I think that thrill-seeking and filling your life with all kinds of adventure tourism are great, but in the end, what you do every day matters significantly more than what you do every once in a while. The biggest payoffs from finding adventure in everything do not come from taking great vacations—although vacations are great—but from upgrading life's more mundane experiences. That is why I believe it is essential that we spend more time appreciating our ordinary days and treating each one like it's a special occasion. Big moments can be found in every hour, every conversation, every meal, and every meeting. You don't have to go on a mountain-climbing expedition in Nepal in order to seize the day or live life to the fullest.

So ignite your spirit of everyday adventure and engage in uncertain pursuits, because life wouldn't be much of an adventure if success was guaranteed. Take a look at your schedule for today and tomorrow and see what kind of adventure the next two days has to offer. Set aside time for your newfound enthusiasm in your everyday life and don't refuse to go on an occasional wild goose chase. Besides, that's what wild geese are for.

Here are some helpful ideas to get you started:

* Say "yes" to literally everything for one weekend
* Build an indoor fort using blankets and sleep in it
* Go on a walk through some nearby woods and take your camera along
* Create a family time capsule and bury it in the backyard
* Have a friend set you up on a blind date
* Start the day with three pennies in your left pocket. Transfer a penny over to your left pocket after a meaningful conversation with someone, and try to end every day with an empty left pocket
* Take a picture every day for a month
* Go a whole day without saying "me" or "I"
* Start having a regular night out with friends
* Meet thirty people in thirty days
* Camp out for a night in the backyard

Everyday Adventure Bucket List

Where do you see potential to include adventure in your schedule?

Everyday Adventure Bucket List

What are simple ways that you can live uniquely?

Everyday Adventure Bucket List

What are simple ways that you can live uniquely?

_____

_____

_____

_____

_____

_____

_____

_____

_____

_____

_____

_____

_____

Everyday Adventure Bucket List

What are simple ways that you can live uniquely?

Everyday Adventure Bucket List

What are simple ways that you can live uniquely?

CREATIVITY BUCKET LIST

CHAPTER 7

Whether you know it or not, there are talents within you right now that you have not yet explored. They are waiting to be unlocked, and in order to do so, you have to exercise your creativity. I believe that it is important to express your uniqueness in a creative way, because by doing so, you communicate a clear message about who you are and how you think. Creativity allows you to see what no one else sees and makes your thoughts visible to others. Sometimes all it takes is making new combinations, connecting the unconnected, looking at the other side, or looking into a new field of interest. Don't sell yourself short just because it doesn't seem like the "creative gene" was passed down to you. Creativity is a gift that you, like everyone else, was born with—a gift that you expressed even before you could talk or use paint, crayons, and building blocks.

I highly encourage you to identify yourself as a creator and do the work you want to see done. Create something unique that you love and, who knows, people may imitate it. Creativity is not something that is limited to the arts, either. It is simply intelligence and talent having fun. It is inventing, experimenting, growing, taking risks, breaking rules, making mistakes, and enjoying it along the way. So often, people tend to let go of their creativity as they grow older, but why? People who live life creatively and spontaneously tend to live abundantly fun-filled and passionate lives, and that is something we can never be too old for. So open yourself up to some creative confidence and be bold with your innovations. Step away from the computer, break the rules, make friends with a different group of people, build something yourself, turn your work into play, and remember that life itself is a work of art.

Here are some helpful ideas to get you started:

* Compile a list of five funny jokes or stories

* Spray-paint your own graffiti mural

* Write an article for a major publication

* Compete in a ballroom dancing competition

* Post a unique YouTube video skit

* Furnish your room or house with something that you've hand-made

* Concoct several new beverages and host a party for friends to try them

* Bake dessert for the family and add your own secret spice

* Find a bucket and design it to illustrate your bucket list

* Attend a pottery or sculpting class

* Write a song and produce it

* Design and develop your own website

* Go above and beyond with your Halloween costume

* Pull off a ridiculously romantic stunt or date

* Splatter-paint a canvas and put it on display in your home

* Volunteer to design a shirt for your next family reunion

Creativity Bucket List

I WANT TO CREATE _____

WHEN _____

HOW _____

_____

WHY _____

_____

_____

· · · · · · · · · · · · · · · ·

I WANT TO CREATE _____

WHEN _____

HOW _____

_____

WHY _____

_____

_____

Creativity Bucket List

I WANT TO CREATE _____

WHEN _____

HOW _____

_____

WHY _____

_____

_____

• • • • • • • • • • • • • • •

I WANT TO CREATE _____

WHEN _____

HOW _____

_____

WHY _____

_____

_____

CREATIVITY BUCKET LIST

I WANT TO CREATE _____

WHEN _____

HOW _____

_____

WHY _____

_____

_____

· · · · · · · · · · · · · · · ·

I WANT TO CREATE _____

WHEN _____

HOW _____

WHY _____

_____

_____

Creativity Bucket List

I WANT TO CREATE _____

WHEN _____

HOW _____

_____

WHY _____

_____

_____

· · · · · · · · · · · · · · · · · ·

I WANT TO CREATE _____

WHEN _____

HOW _____

_____

WHY _____

_____

_____

Creativity Bucket List

I WANT TO CREATE _____

WHEN _____

HOW _____

_____

WHY _____

_____

_____

. . . .

I WANT TO CREATE _____

WHEN _____

HOW _____

_____

WHY _____

_____

_____

Creativity Bucket List

I WANT TO CREATE _____

WHEN _____

HOW _____

_____

WHY _____

_____

_____

· · · · · · · · · · · · · ·

I WANT TO CREATE _____

WHEN _____

HOW _____

_____

WHY _____

_____

_____

CREATIVITY BUCKET LIST

I WANT TO CREATE _____

WHEN _____

HOW _____

_____

WHY _____

_____

_____

· · · · · · · · · · · · · · · ·

I WANT TO CREATE _____

WHEN _____

HOW _____

_____

WHY _____

_____

_____

Travel Bucket List

CHAPTER 8

You may be comfortable with where you are right now—comfortable with the people around you and the familiarity of your own city—but I cannot emphasize enough the importance of traveling. It should be on everyone's bucket list. Whether it involves spending several days on another continent, backpacking in the countryside with friends, or just getting outside of the city and going on a road trip with family, every adventure is worthwhile. When exploring new ground and trying new things, all other burdens seem to slip away, and a therapeutic contentment often follows as a result of a diminishing preoccupation with oneself.

Do not be mistaken: I do not see traveling as a method for escaping life, but rather I see it as a method to ensure that life does not escape you. In my eyes, it has nothing to do with gear or footwear or the backpacking fads, or even with getting from point A to point B. No, the beauty is in the walking. Traveling is about the discovery of new cultures and ideas in foreign lands. It's about the feeling of letting go and doing things differently than ever before. It's about jamming a stick in the spokes of your routine, and it's about finding a place that feeds you—creatively, socially, spiritually, and (of course) literally.

Without new experiences, something inside of us sleeps. There is so much to see, and not nearly enough time to witness it all, so travel far and wide, travel boldly, and travel with full abandon. Wherever it is that you dream of going, do not let price, language, or distance keep you from taking your first steps in that direction. Make a new path, travel the extra mile, and go to the edge.

Here are some helpful ideas to get you started:

* ✳ Visit one of the modern wonders of the world
* ✳ Set foot in four different continents
* ✳ Travel by camel
* ✳ Touch sand and snow within one day of each other
* ✳ Tour the Colosseum
* ✳ See the Northern Lights
* ✳ Throw a dart at a map of your country and go to wherever it lands
* ✳ Venture on a safari
* ✳ Get a picture in front of ten different state welcome signs
* ✳ Camp out in a national park
* ✳ Hit the slots in Las Vegas
* ✳ Spend New Year's Eve in Times Square
* ✳ Backpack across a continent and keep a travel journal
* ✳ Take a week-long road trip with friends
* ✳ Drive to the mountains for a mountain-biking trip
* ✳ Get your motorcycle license and map out a road trip with a friend
* ✳ Sign up for a mission trip in a third-world country
* ✳ Photograph and document your travels through the rainforest

Travel Bucket List

Ideas to get you started:

1. Which countries do you want to explore?

2. Research three cities that you would like to visit in a country.

3. Dream up an itinerary of foods to try, sights to see, and activities to participate in for those three cities.

4. Go!

Travel Plans

I want to travel to _____

I would like to go there because _____

_____

When _____

When I am there, I would like to see _____

_____

_____

_____

Travel Bucket List

I want to travel to _____

I would like to go there because _____

_____

When _____

When I am there, I would like to see _____

_____

_____

_____

· · · · · · · · · · · · · · · ·

I want to travel to _____

I would like to go there because _____

_____

When _____

When I am there, I would like to see _____

_____

_____

_____

Travel Bucket List

I want to travel to _____

I would like to go there because _____

_____

When _____

When I am there, I would like to see _____

_____

_____

_____

· · · · · · · · · · · · · · · · · ·

I want to travel to _____

I would like to go there because _____

_____

When _____

When I am there, I would like to see _____

_____

_____

_____

Travel Bucket List

I want to travel to _____

I would like to go there because _____

_____

When _____

When I am there, I would like to see _____

_____

_____

_____

· ·

I want to travel to _____

I would like to go there because _____

_____

When _____

When I am there, I would like to see _____

_____

_____

_____

Travel Bucket List

I want to travel to _____

I would like to go there because _____

_____

When _____

When I am there, I would like to see _____

_____

_____

_____

• • • • • • • • • • • • • • • • • •

I want to travel to _____

I would like to go there because _____

_____

When _____

When I am there, I would like to see _____

_____

_____

_____

Travel Bucket List

I want to travel to _____

I would like to go there because _____

_____

When _____

When I am there, I would like to see _____

_____

_____

_____

· · · · · · · · · · · · · · · · ·

I want to travel to _____

I would like to go there because _____

_____

When _____

When I am there, I would like to see _____

_____

_____

_____

Travel Bucket List

I want to travel to _____

I would like to go there because _____

_____

When _____

When I am there, I would like to see _____

_____

_____

_____

· · · · · · · · · · · · · · · · · · · ·

I want to travel to _____

I would like to go there because _____

_____

When _____

When I am there, I would like to see _____

_____

_____

QUITTER BUCKET LIST

CHAPTER 9

I've got a challenge for you: try to go the next twenty-four hours without complaining. Though it may sound easy, this is one of those sneaky bad habits that somehow works its way into nearly everyone's day. Even if you're not a big complainer, you're likely to catch yourself spouting out negative complaints at least a handful of times. Just like the habit of complaining, a majority of habits develop unintentionally. At the beginning, they form a kind of invisible thread, and through repetition, that thread becomes entwined into a cord and later into a rope. Each time an act is repeated, we add to and strengthen it. Although habits can be used as fantastic tools for success, they can also be destructive and cause unwanted problems. So while the other bucket lists encourage you to seek out new goals to conquer, a Quitter Bucket List encourages you to set goals for quitting.

Although it uses a different approach, a Quitter Bucket List focuses on self-improvement, just like the other bucket lists. Whether you are trying to lose weight, struggling to reduce laziness, or aiming to lower stress levels, the point of a this list is to make sustainable changes to kick bad habits. Just starting with a tiny decision has the potential to eliminate a lot of wasted time. With this list, you don't have to worry about maintaining the quality of your life, because every day you will work on improving it. Try developing an idea of how you're going to make changes for yourself in the weeks and months to come, and then you might find it helpful to get a wall calendar that you can break into daily chunks. For each day that you have managed to refrain from your designated bad habits, make a big fat X in that day's box After a couple days, you'll develop a feeling of pride for each of those big Xs, and once you've got a chain, your only job is to not break it.

You don't need an absurd amount of willpower to quit any of these habits; you just need to start with the desire. It is also helpful to note that substituting a habit is much more effective than quitting a habit cold turkey. Rather than trying to just quit stress, try to replace it with quick meditative breathing skills. And don't forget to specify your short-, mid-, and long-term goals and additional considerations to achieve the outcome. Whether it is a habit that you need to quit or just a habit that you are interested in quitting once, know that our habits reflect our characters and have the potential to teach us volumes about ourselves. If there is a habit that you are ready to get rid of, then add it to your list today. The bad habits may be stronger than you thought, but the rewards will be bigger than you think, so start tackling your Quitter Bucket list today, and make sure that you kick the habit long before you kick the bucket.

TIP: It is also helpful to know that quitting is best begun on a Thursday. Since the majority of bad habits are usually rampant during the weekends. Starting on a Thursday will give you enough willpower to make it through the toughest part: the first weekend.

Quitter Bucket List

I want to quit _____

Why I need to do this _____

_____

When _____

How I am going remove this from my life _____

_____

Accomplished ○

· · · · · · · · · · · · · · · · ·

I want to quit _____

Why I need to do this _____

_____

When _____

How I am going remove this from my life _____

_____

Accomplished ○

Quitter Bucket List

I want to quit _____

Why I need to do this _____

_____

When _____

How I am going remove this from my life _____

_____

Accomplished ⃝

· · · · · · · · · · · · · · · · · ·

I want to quit _____

Why I need to do this _____

_____

When _____

How I am going remove this from my life _____

_____

Accomplished ⃝

Quitter Bucket List

I want to quit _____

Why I need to do this _____

_____

When _____

How I am going remove this from my life _____

_____

Accomplished ○

· · · · · · · · · · · · · · · · ·

I want to quit _____

Why I need to do this _____

_____

When _____

How I am going remove this from my life _____

_____

Accomplished ○

Quitter Bucket List

I want to quit _____

Why I need to do this _____

_____

When _____

How I am going remove this from my life _____

_____

Accomplished ◯

• • • • • • • • • • • • • • • • •

I want to quit _____

Why I need to do this _____

_____

When _____

How I am going remove this from my life _____

_____

Accomplished ◯

Quitter Bucket List

I want to quit _____

Why I need to do this _____

_____

When _____

How I am going remove this from my life _____

_____

Accomplished ◯

· · · · · · · · · · · · · · · · · ·

I want to quit _____

Why I need to do this _____

_____

When _____

How I am going remove this from my life _____

_____

Accomplished ◯

Quitter Bucket List

I want to quit _____

Why I need to do this _____

_____

When _____

How I am going remove this from my life _____

_____

Accomplished ◯

· · · · · · · · · · · · · · · · · ·

I want to quit _____

Why I need to do this _____

_____

When _____

How I am going remove this from my life _____

_____

Accomplished ◯

Quitter Bucket List

I want to quit _____

Why I need to do this _____

_____

When _____

How I am going remove this from my life _____

_____

Accomplished ◯

· ·

I want to quit _____

Why I need to do this _____

_____

When _____

How I am going remove this from my life _____

_____

Accomplished ◯

Summer Bucket List

CHAPTER 10

If you've ever tried to motivate yourself to accomplish something during the summertime, you've probably realized that goals without a deadline are a lot like objectives without a plan; if you don't have a set timeframe for the end result, it becomes much more tempting to procrastinate. No matter how difficult the task, the amount of work often expands to fill the time available for its completion, making those easy two-hour tasks seem a lot more daunting and stressful when given a week or two to complete them. But because of this, deadlines can also be used as incredible tools for motivation, and that's why I think it is important to have a deadline on your Summer Bucket List.

The best strategy that I have found to conceptualize the remaining time is by using a jar of marbles. Rather than crossing off days from the calendar, count out the number of days left in your summer and place them in a jar. Every day, as you wake up, pull one marble out and keep it with you throughout the day as a reminder of the importance of investing your time in the places that matter. My hope is that this method will keep you more focused on the journey toward your goals rather than on the goals themselves, and that each marble in your pocket will keep you from bingeing on all but one thing: life itself. Understand that losing a marble each day is inevitable, but also keep in mind that you get to decide where it goes and how it is invested. The jar will stand as a constant token of the number of days that you have left, and each marble will serve as a catalyst for motivation. Remember, a successful summer is not achieved after just one fun weekend trip or one memorable experience; it can only be achieved by spending a summer's worth of marbles in the right way. As soon as all of the little marbles start adding up, we begin working with time instead of against it. It is my belief that everyone should have some sort of reminder to measure their days and encourage lifelong curiosity. Some use calendars; some use journals; I use a jar of marbles. How will you measure your life?

Use the space below to calculate the number of days left in your summer and think up several ways to measure the time that you have left. Jot down some upcoming goals with deadlines that you may have and make sure that your jar is somewhere that you often look.

Summer Bucket List

This summer I would like to _____

_____

I would like to do this because _____

_____

_____

When _____

_____

Accomplished ○

· · · · · · · · · · · · · · · · ·

This summer I would like to _____

_____

I would like to do this because _____

_____

_____

When _____

_____

Accomplished ○

Summer Bucket List

This summer I would like to _____

_____

I would like to do this because _____

_____

_____

When _____

_____

Accomplished ○

· · · · · · · · · · · · · · · · · ·

This summer I would like to _____

_____

I would like to do this because _____

_____

_____

When _____

_____

Accomplished ○

Summer Bucket List

This summer I would like to _____

_____

I would like to do this because _____

_____

_____

When _____

_____

Accomplished ◯

• • • • • • • • • • • • • • • • • •

This summer I would like to _____

_____

I would like to do this because _____

_____

_____

When _____

_____

Accomplished ◯

Summer Bucket List

This summer I would like to _____

_____

I would like to do this because _____

_____

_____

When _____

_____

Accomplished ◯

• • • • • • • • • • • • • • •

This summer I would like to _____

_____

I would like to do this because _____

_____

_____

When _____

_____

Accomplished ◯

Summer Bucket List

This summer I would like to _____

_____

I would like to do this because _____

_____

_____

When _____

_____

Accomplished ◯

• • • • • • • • • • • • • • •

This summer I would like to _____

_____

I would like to do this because _____

_____

_____

When _____

_____

Accomplished ◯

REVERSE BUCKET LIST

CHAPTER 11

Too much focus on future goals and incomplete bucket list items can be daunting and even stressful. That's why every so often, rather than adding more unfinished goals to the list, I take a backward look at everything I have already done and focus only on the wonderful experiences that my life has been filled with. Many of the highlights of my life weren't planned and researched; they just happened. And I believe that these moments should be celebrated, too. This is why I recommend that everyone create a Reverse Bucket List.

The way that this list works is by taking stock of everything you have accomplished instead of writing down everything you have left to do. These are accomplishments that you may not have had on your bucket list up to this point but are items that are still worth mentioning and worth writing down retroactively. You may notice that these milestones are less conspicuous than other bucket list items because they often come to the door of memory unannounced. But you may also find that these are the milestones that you are most proud of and the ones that make for the best stories. I find it funny how quick we are to write off things we've done in the past and only focus on all the things we want for the future. We study mechanically to pass exams, we work around the clock for the next promotion, and we pick ourselves up from failure time and time again, but we rarely remember to reward ourselves along the way. If we don't pay attention to the more subtle accomplishments, then we will live in what seems like a world of limited celebration.

The point is not to be worried about getting ahead, but simply to be ecstatic about having accumulated so many great memories. Although this list is great for boosting confidence, know that it is not intended for bragging rights, but rather for a bit of reflection on the past and for remembrance to stay focused on the positive. I challenge you to compile a list of at least 30 past accomplishments and construct your own Reverse Bucket List. When you're done, celebrate the routine, the ridiculous, and the personal victories that have brought you to where you are today. Then break out the rocky road ice cream for a sweet celebration.

1. I ACCOMPLISHED _____

DATE _____

I AM HAPPY ABOUT THIS BECAUSE _____

_____

2. I ACCOMPLISHED _____

DATE _____

I AM HAPPY ABOUT THIS BECAUSE _____

_____

3. I accomplished _____

DATE _____

I am happy about this because _____

_____

4. I accomplished _____

DATE _____

I am happy about this because _____

_____

5. I accomplished _____

DATE _____

I am happy about this because _____

_____

6. I accomplished _____

DATE _____

I am happy about this because _____

_____

Reverse Bucket List

7. I accomplished _____

DATE _____

I am happy about this because _____

_____

8. I accomplished _____

DATE _____

I am happy about this because _____

_____

9. I accomplished _____

DATE _____

I am happy about this because _____

_____

10. I accomplished _____

DATE _____

I am happy about this because _____

_____

11. I accomplished _____

date _____

I am happy about this because _____

_____

12. I accomplished _____

date _____

I am happy about this because _____

_____

13. I accomplished _____

date _____

I am happy about this because _____

_____

14. I accomplished _____

date _____

I am happy about this because _____

_____

Reverse Bucket List

15. I accomplished _____

DATE _____

I am happy about this because _____

_____

16. I accomplished _____

DATE _____

I am happy about this because _____

_____

17. I accomplished _____

DATE _____

I am happy about this because _____

_____

18. I accomplished _____

DATE _____

I am happy about this because _____

_____

Reverse Bucket List

19. I accomplished _____

DATE _____

I AM HAPPY ABOUT THIS BECAUSE _____

_____

20. I accomplished _____

DATE _____

I AM HAPPY ABOUT THIS BECAUSE _____

_____

21. I accomplished _____

DATE _____

I AM HAPPY ABOUT THIS BECAUSE _____

_____

22. I accomplished _____

DATE _____

I AM HAPPY ABOUT THIS BECAUSE _____

_____

Reverse Bucket List

23. I accomplished _____

DATE _____

I am happy about this because _____

24. I accomplished _____

DATE _____

I am happy about this because _____

25. I accomplished _____

DATE _____

I am happy about this because _____

26. I accomplished _____

DATE _____

I am happy about this because _____

27. I accomplished _____

DATE _____

I am happy about this because _____

_____

28. I accomplished _____

DATE _____

I am happy about this because _____

_____

29. I accomplished _____

DATE _____

I am happy about this because _____

_____

30. I accomplished _____

DATE _____

I am happy about this because _____

_____

Radical Bucket List

CHAPTER 12

Many of us have dreams that we keep to ourselves—dreams that we give up on prematurely after telling ourselves that we don't have the courage to follow through with them; dreams that seem so outrageous that we never dare to write them down on paper for fear that we might be called crazy. It's human nature to want to explore, to find a line and want to go beyond it. There can be a strange thrill of accomplishment, a self-congratulatory sensation, when doing something radical, like skydiving, even when it's completely unwarranted. Simply letting gravity take control as you tempt nature by jumping out of an aircraft can fill you with such a rush that you believe you can achieve anything. The same goes for cliff jumping, especially when the jump is high enough to take your breath away as you plunge beneath the warmer water at the top, down to where it's dark and cold at the bottom—so cold that it sends you gasping back for the surface and the sun. After that first jump, you have to do it again, partly because you can't believe you did it and partly because the fear has given way to the thrill of such freedom.

I think that a bucket list specifically designed for radical living can be significant. It allows us to reach as high as we want and reminds us to venture toward all of our dreams and passions instead of just the safe ones. I'm not saying that you should build a bucket list filled with eighteen different versions of Russian roulette, but I am saying that it may require you to redefine the parameters of your comfort zone. Remember, no one is born with courage; sometimes all you need is ten seconds of insane courage or ten seconds of embarrassing bravery.

Now, I am asking you to step up and put your greatest desires on the page. If you had permission to do what you really wanted to do, what would you do? Don't ask how—that will cut your desire off at the knees. Our lives really can be the great adventure we so passionately want them to be. Wouldn't you rather live a life of "oh wells" than a life of "what ifs," and besides, the most dangerous risk of all is the risk of spending your life not doing what you want on the bet that you can buy yourself the freedom to do it later.

Swim with sharks, tackle a marathon, jump out of a helicopter with nothing but a pair of skis on your feet, go crowd surfing, breathe fire, bungee jump off a bridge, race a sports car, test your luck in catfish noodling, saddle up on a bull, kayak down a waterfall, participate in an open-mic night at a comedy club, or camp out in the wilderness with nothing but a knife, a flint rock, and the clothes on your back. Pick the thing you are most afraid of and conquer it.

Now it's your turn. Dream big!

Radical Bucket List

My radical dream is to _____

I would like to do this because _____

When am I going to do this _____

Steps I need to take to make this happen _____

_____

_____

_____

_____

· · · · · · · · · · · · · · · · · ·

My radical dream is to _____

I would like to do this because _____

When am I going to do this _____

Steps I need to take to make this happen _____

_____

_____

_____

_____

Radical Bucket List

My radical dream is to _____

I would like to do this because _____

When am I going to do this _____

Steps I need to take to make this happen _____

_____

_____

_____

· · · · · · · · · · · · · · · ·

My radical dream is to _____

I would like to do this because _____

When am I going to do this _____

Steps I need to take to make this happen _____

_____

_____

_____

Radical Bucket List

My radical dream is to _____

I would like to do this because _____

When am I going to do this _____

Steps I need to take to make this happen _____

_____

_____

_____

· ·

My radical dream is to _____

I would like to do this because _____

When am I going to do this _____

Steps I need to take to make this happen _____

_____

_____

_____

Radical Bucket List

My radical dream is to _____

I would like to do this because _____

When am I going to do this _____

Steps I need to take to make this happen _____

_____

_____

_____

· · · · · · · · · · · · · · · · · ·

My radical dream is to _____

I would like to do this because _____

When am I going to do this _____

Steps I need to take to make this happen _____

_____

_____

_____

Radical Bucket List

My radical dream is to _____

I would like to do this because _____

When am I going to do this _____

Steps I need to take to make this happen _____

_____

_____

_____

· · · · · · · · · · · · · · · · · ·

My radical dream is to _____

I would like to do this because _____

When am I going to do this _____

Steps I need to take to make this happen _____

_____

_____

_____

ENDNOTE

Though we've reached the end, I don't consider this book finished. Now is the time for you to start pursuing all of the adventures that you have written down and stop wearing your wishbone where your backbone ought to be. Great change doesn't just come with an official endorsement, and you don't have to feel like you have been struck by lightning to start following your dreams. Start making a ritual of scanning the items on your list and updating yourself on the progress you have made toward achieving each goal. When you are looking for more willpower, challenge yourself with your Quitter Bucket List, and if you ever need encouragement, crack open your Reverse Bucket List. In the summer, pull out your Summer Bucket List, and in seasons of hardship redirect yourself with your Spiritual Bucket List.

Learn something new every day, explore your creative side, get obsessed, get radical, live with compassion, enjoy the little things, find adventure in everything you do, and have fun.

ABOUT THE AUTHOR